Contents

Chapter 1

A LIVING PLANET

In pictures of Earth taken from outer space, you can see the planet's blue oceans, vast deserts, dark green forests, and white clouds. Earth is unlike any other place in the solar system. Earth is full of life. It is home to billions of plants, animals, and people. Humans know more about Earth than any other planet. That's because it is our home planet.

A satellite took this picture of clouds swirling over North and South America. The satellite tracks weather conditions in this part of the planet.

The solar system has eight planets, which orbit the sun. Mercury is the closest planet to the sun. The next closest is Venus and then Earth, Mars, Jupiter, Saturn, Uranus, and Neptune.

The time it takes a planet to make one full orbit around the sun is called a year. A year on Earth is a little more than 365 days. Earth also spins like a top. One full rotation takes twenty-four hours, or a day.

As Earth spins, part of the planet faces toward the sun while the other part faces away from the sun. The side facing the sun has daytime while the other side has night.

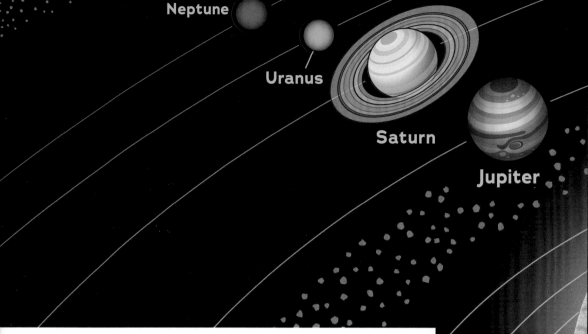

Neptune

Uranus

Saturn

Jupiter

Planets get heat and light from the sun. The planets closest to the sun are burning hot. The planets farther away are bitterly cold. Earth is in between. Its average temperature is 61°F (16°C).

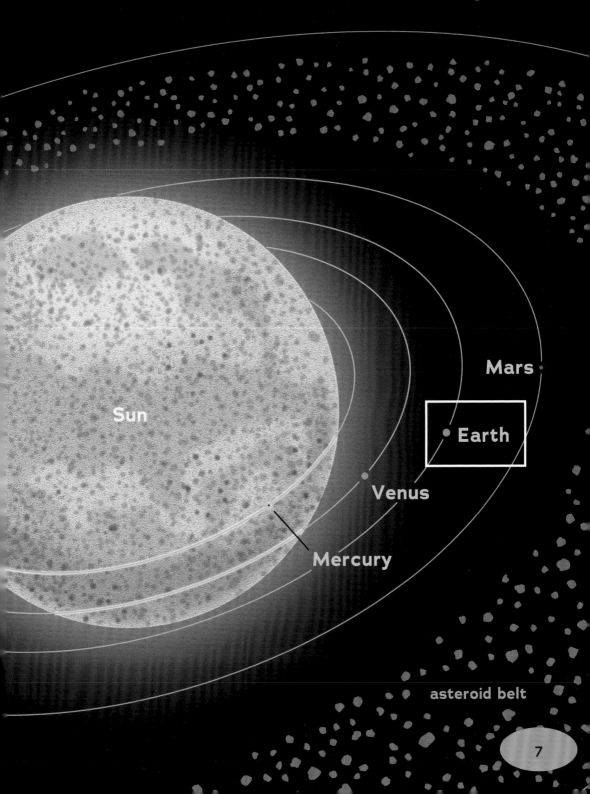

The Solar System

Mars

Sun

Earth

Venus

Mercury

asteroid belt

A Full Moon

A moon is a large natural object that orbits a planet. Earth has one moon. It orbits Earth about once a month. The moon rotates too. It spins once every 29.5 days.

The moon is the brightest object in the night sky. But it doesn't give off its own light. Instead, it reflects light from the sun. When the sun lights up one whole side of the moon, we call it a full moon. Sometimes we can see only part of the moon. The shape we see changes as the moon orbits Earth.

The sun lights only part of the moon in this image. We see a full moon about once each month.

STEM Highlight

The moon has always fascinated humans. In the 1960s, humans explored the moon up close for the first time. They sent spacecraft to the moon. Astronauts flew to the moon in the 1960s and 1970s. Some of them walked on the moon's surface. They took photographs and collected moon rocks and soil. Some astronauts explored the moon on carts. The missions helped astronomers learn more about the moon's gravity, what the moon is made of, and how it formed.

Astronaut Edwin "Buzz" Aldrin stands on the moon's surface in 1969.

INSIDE AND OUT

If you wanted to travel to the middle of Earth, you'd have a long way to go. It's about 3,963 miles (6,378 km) from Earth's surface to its center, or core. Earth's core is a hot ball of iron and nickel.

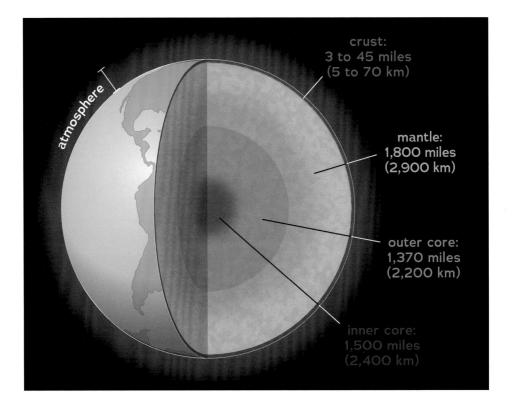

atmosphere

crust:
3 to 45 miles
(5 to 70 km)

mantle:
1,800 miles
(2,900 km)

outer core:
1,370 miles
(2,200 km)

inner core:
1,500 miles
(2,400 km)

The core has two sections. The inner core is solid metal. The outer core is liquid metal. The hottest part of the core is where the inner and outer core meet. There, it is about 10,800°F (6,000°C). That's about as hot as the surface of the sun.

A thick layer of rock surrounds the core. This layer is Earth's mantle. Heat from the core melts some of the rock in the mantle. Sometimes melted rock flows up and pushes through Earth's surface. This is a volcano.

HOT, MELTED ROCKS FLOW DOWN THE SIDE OF AN ACTIVE VOLCANO IN ECUADOR.

Surf and Turf

Earth's outer layer is the crust. This rocky layer contains all the dry land on Earth. The land beneath the oceans is also part of Earth's crust. So are mountain ranges, deep canyons, and other land formations. Water covers more than 70 percent of Earth's surface. The rest of the surface is dry land.

This image of Earth's surface, taken from space, shows a sea, rivers, and mountains.

STEM Highlight

Earth's crust is like a cracked eggshell. It has about thirty pieces, called tectonic plates. They move a few inches each year.

Sometimes two tectonic plates bump into each other, and the ground pushes up. Over millions of years, as the plates keep pressing together, the ground moves more. It becomes a mountain. Other times, a plate moves suddenly and the ground shakes. This is an earthquake. Sometimes two plates move away from each other. That leaves a trench between the plates. Volcanoes might erupt through the trench.

Along with the movement of tectonic plates, wind, rain, and ice shape mountains over time.

The Life Force

Animals and plants live almost everywhere on Earth. Earth is a welcoming place for living things. It is the only planet known to have life.

Earth's distance from the sun is just right for life. If Earth were closer to the sun, it would be too hot for most  living things. If it were farther from the sun, it would be too cold. Earth also has lots of water. Plants and animals need water to live.

Earth's rain forests hold more than half of the plants and animals found on the planet.

Earth's atmosphere is a layer of gases around the planet. The atmosphere contains the air that living things breathe. The atmosphere traps heat so Earth doesn't get too cold. It also protects living things from the sun's harmful rays.

The atmosphere has five layers. The troposphere is closest to the ground. Most weather happens in the troposphere. The stratosphere is above the troposphere. Next come the mesosphere, the thermosphere, and the exosphere. The exosphere is where the atmosphere blends with outer space. It begins about 310 miles (500 km) above Earth.

This image shot from space shows some of the layers of Earth's atmosphere. The orange layer is the troposphere. The stratosphere begins where the sky becomes blue.

Chapter 3

INQUIRING MINDS

Since ancient times, humans have been curious about
the world around them. People looked up into the night sky
and wanted to know about the universe. They explored the
areas where they lived and wanted to know about Earth.
They made maps and measurements. Many ancient
people thought the world was flat. They also believed

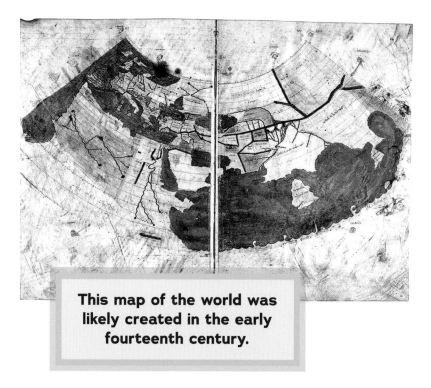

**This map of the world was
likely created in the early
fourteenth century.**

Earth was the center of the universe. Scientists and astronomers studied the world and watched the skies to learn more.

Aristotle was a scientist and philosopher who lived more than two thousand years ago in Greece. He believed Earth was round. He saw that when ships sailed far away, they seemed to sink and then disappear. This happened, Aristotle said, because the ships traveled over Earth's curved surface. They disappeared from view as they sailed down the curve.

When a ship sails away, it appears to become smaller and smaller and then sink over the horizon. If Earth were flat, the ship would not appear to sink.

About one hundred years later, a Greek scientist name Eratosthenes noticed that in one city in Egypt, on one day a year, the sun was directly overhead at noon. Objects there did not cast a shadow. At the same time in another city, the sun was not right overhead. Its rays hit Earth at an angle, making shadows. Eratosthenes measured the angles of the shadows. He used this information to figure out how much Earth curved. Then he figured out the distance between the two cities. Once he knew that, he calculated the distance around the entire planet.

Exploring Orbits

In the sixteenth century, Polish astronomer Nicolaus Copernicus wrote that Earth and the other planets circled the sun. Italian astronomer Galileo Galilei agreed with Copernicus. He watched the motion of planets through a telescope. He knew the planets would move differently if they were orbiting Earth. Soon most scientists agreed that planets orbit around the sun.

Copernicus wrote a book about his idea that the planets circle the sun. It was published in 1543, the same year Copernicus died.

ISAAC NEWTON WAS A SCIENTIST WHO MADE DISCOVERIES ABOUT GRAVITY, LIGHT, AND COLOR.

In the 1660s, Isaac Newton, a British scientist, studied gravity. Earth's gravity pulls objects toward the ground. Newton said that Earth's gravity pulls on the moon. This pull helps keep the moon in orbit around Earth. Gravity also keeps the planets in orbit around the sun.

Seeing Earth from Space

In 1957, people sent the first satellite, *Sputnik 1*, into orbit around Earth. It was about the size of a beach ball. *Sputnik 1* gathered information about the upper layers of Earth's atmosphere.

The Soviet Union, a former nation based in modern-day Russia, launched *Sputnik 1*. The event led to the launch of many more spacecraft.

A robotic arm releases a satellite into Earth's orbit in 2016.

After *Sputnik 1*, scientists sent many more satellites into space. Many satellites carry scientific instruments. Some instruments measure Earth's winds, temperatures, and other weather features. Other instruments map land formations, rivers, and oceans. Cameras on satellites take photographs of Earth. These satellites help scientists understand more about Earth's atmosphere and landscape.

STEM Highlight

Scientists wanted to know Earth's age. In the early twentieth century, scientists began studying the age of rocks all over Earth. They found rocks that were more than 3 billion years old. Scientists also studied moon rocks and meteorites. These rocks were as old as 4.5 billion years.

Scientists believe the whole solar system formed at the same time. But over time, Earth's oldest rocks broke down, melted, or became buried. Since the meteorites are about 4.5 billion years old, scientists think Earth is 4.5 billion years old too.

The last two astronauts to explore the moon found this boulder on the moon's surface in 1972.

Chapter 4

DIGGING DEEPER

Humans have been studying Earth for thousands of years, but there is a lot more to learn about our home planet. In 2014, scientists found a watery area in Earth's mantle. The area may hold more water than all Earth's oceans combined. The water sits in the mantle below the United States. Other parts of the mantle might have water too. But scientists have not found it yet.

This image shows a sample of ringwoodite, the mineral that holds water in Earth's mantle.

Water Everywhere

If you could visit the bottom of Earth's oceans, you'd find tall underwater mountains and deep underwater canyons. Scientists have used many kinds of technology to study the ocean floor. But the oceans cover almost 140 million square miles (363 million sq. km) of Earth. Scientists have mapped only about 5 percent of the ocean floor.

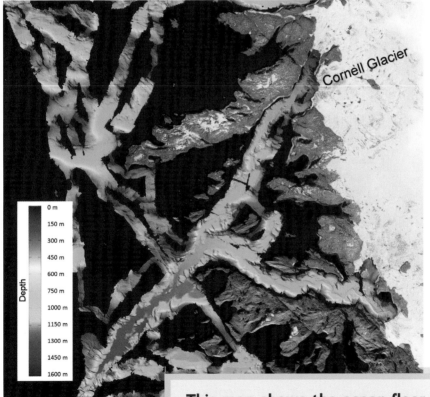

Cornell Glacier

Depth

0 m
150 m
300 m
450 m
600 m
750 m
1000 m
1150 m
1300 m
1450 m
1600 m

This map shows the ocean floor off the coast of Greenland.

The ocean floor is filled with caves such as this one. Seabed 2030 hopes to map all of the ocean floor's features.

A project called Seabed 2030 started in 2017. The project uses sound waves to map the ocean floor. The waves hit the seafloor and bounce back. Computers analyze the returning sound waves. They figure out the depth of the water in each spot. By combining the measurements, computers can make a map of the ocean floor. Project leaders hope to map the whole ocean by the year 2030.

Hot Spot

Human actions are changing Earth. People cut down trees, build up cities, and move into areas where animals once lived. People burn oil, coal, and natural gas to heat homes and to run cars and other machines. These activities release carbon dioxide into the air. Extra carbon dioxide traps extra heat, so Earth is getting hotter.

Scientists are tracking the changes on Earth. They measure temperatures and study plants and animals. These scientists want to keep Earth safe and healthy so plants, people, and animals can continue to live on the planet.

In the United States, vehicle pollution is one of the biggest ways humans release carbon dioxide into the air.

STEM Highlight

In 1998, scientists began building the International Space Station (ISS) in outer space. In 2000, the first astronauts went to live on the ISS. Since then, many astronauts have gone to the ISS to conduct experiments that help us understand Earth and the human body.

On the ISS, gravity is not as strong as it is on Earth. Astronauts there study how gravity affects living things. Astronauts study plants in space. They test new medicines and use robots and cameras to study Earth from space. These experiments help scientists learn more about Earth and plan for future missions in outer space.

Astronaut Peggy Whitson shows soybeans growing on the ISS. The experiment studies how gravity affects seeds and plant growth.

Looking Ahead

- Scientists are tracking changes to Earth's weather and temperatures. Earth is getting too warm for some plants and animals. If temperatures keep rising, food crops might not grow. Many people might go hungry.

- Does life exist any place besides Earth? Scientists think that Mars might have had life in the past. Scientists want to explore other planets and moons to learn more about how life began.

- Where did Earth's water come from? Scientists have two theories. One is that a meteorite carried water to Earth from somewhere else in space. Another is that Earth's water formed when the planet formed. Scientists are studying Earth's mantle, meteorites, and other planets to answer the question.

Glossary

astronaut: a person who is trained to travel beyond Earth's atmosphere. Astronauts have orbited Earth in spacecraft and visited the moon.

astronomer: a person who studies objects and forces outside Earth's atmosphere, such as planets, stars, and energy traveling through space

atmosphere: a layer of gases surrounding a planet, a moon, or another object in space

gravity: a force that pulls objects toward one another

meteorite: a piece of rock or metal from outer space that crashes into Earth

orbit: to travel around another object in an oval or circular path

rotate: to spin around like a top

satellite: an object that orbits Earth or another body in space

solar system: a star and the planets and other objects that orbit it. The sun is the star in our solar system.

tectonic plate: one of about thirty large pieces that make up Earth's crust

telescope: an instrument that makes distant objects look bigger

Learn More about Earth

Books

Storad, Conrad J. *Uncovering Earth's Crust.* Minneapolis: Lerner Publications, 2013. Why does Earth have tall mountains and underwater volcanoes? Learn all about Earth's crust to find the answers.

Taylor-Butler, Christine. *Planet Earth.* New York: Children's Press, 2014. Read more about the reasons Earth is suited for life and how scientists have made discoveries about Earth and our solar system.

Woodward, John. *Super Earth Encyclopedia.* New York: DK, 2017. Look deep into Earth's interior, high into the atmosphere, and out into the solar system to learn more about our home planet.

Websites

Climate Kids

https://climatekids.nasa.gov

Learn more about how the weather, air, and oceans on Earth are changing, and find games, projects, and tips about taking care of our planet.

Earth

https://spaceplace.nasa.gov/menu/earth/

Play games and complete puzzles to learn more about Earth, the moon, and the solar system.

Journey to the Centre of the Earth

http://www.bbc.com/future/bespoke/story/20150306-journey-to-the
-centre-of-earth/

Do you want to know about the planet beneath your feet? This website takes you on a journey downward—all the way to Earth's core.

Index

Photo Acknowledgments

The images in this book are used with the permission of: NASA/JPL, pp. 4, 5, 8, 9, 12, 15, 21, 22, 23, 28; © Laura Westlund/Independent Picture Service, pp. 6–7, 10; Dr Morley Read/Shutterstock .com, p. 11; Iness Arna/Shutterstock.com, p. 13; Radek Borovka/Shutterstock.com, p. 14; Wikimedia Commons (PD), p. 16; Georgios Tsichlis/Shutterstock.com, p. 17; Imagno/Hulton Archive/Getty Images, p. 18; iryna1/Shutterstock.com, pp. 19, 20; THIERRY ZOCCOLAN/AFP/Getty Images, p. 24; NASA/JPL-Caltech, p. 25; 7maru/Shutterstock.com, p. 26; Savvapanf Photo/Shutterstock.com, p. 27.

Front cover: NASA/JPL.